# Colonial American Home Life

JNO. W. EHNINGER.

# Colonial American

**HOME LIFE**

## by John F. Warner

COLONIAL AMERICA

**FRANKLIN WATTS**

NEW YORK / CHICAGO / LONDON / TORONTO / SYDNEY

Photographs copyright ©: North Wind picture Archives,
Alfred, Me.: pp. 2, 20, 26, 30, 38, 84, 105, 107; New York Public
Library, Picture Collection: pp. 10, 12, 79, 82; The Bettmann
Archive: pp. 18, 22, 32, 34, 43, 45, 48, 52, 55, 57, 65, 67, 73, 74, 76, 91,
94, 96, 100, 102, 112; Historical Pictures/Stock Montage, Chicago,
Ill.: pp. 29, 47, 63; UPI/Bettmann Newsphotos: p. 36; The
Jamestown Foundation: pp. 110, 111.

Library of Congress Cataloging-in-Publication Data

Warner, John F.
Colonial American home life/John F. Warner.
p.   cm.—(Colonial America)
Includes bibliographical references and index.
Summary: Discusses why people settled in the American colonies
and describes aspects of their daily lives, including homes, clothing,
food, work, school, and amusements.
ISBN 0-531-12541-6
1.United States—Social life and customs—To 1775—Juvenile
literature. [1. United States—Social life and customs—To 1775.]
I. Title. II. Series.
E162.W37  1993
973.2—dc20                                              93–3963 CIP AC

6

For Kathleen, Norann, Margaret, and Judd—
pilgrims in their own right

# Acknowledgments

Special thanks to Laurence and Irene Swinburne, colleagues and friends, for their invaluable counsel and assistance

# Contents

# Colonial American Home Life

The early colonists carved
homes out of the wilderness.

# Introduction

Think for a moment about all the things we take for granted in our lives. Most Americans live in houses or apartments, with running water and indoor bathrooms. There are lights to push back the darkness, heat to ward off the cold, perhaps even air conditioning to keep us comfortable on the warmest days.

Buses may take us to and from school. There we have a chance to learn about our world. We can learn, too, about other lands, other peoples, other times.

Telephones, satellites, and computers make it easy to talk to friends and to people far away. There are books, movies, television, and radio to entertain us. And most of us have some time to enjoy these activities.

There are some stores in which to buy food and others to buy clothing, stores that cater to our basic needs and stores that offer luxuries still unknown in many other countries.

There are police officers and fire fighters to protect us, and doctors and nurses to help us when we are sick

Bark huts, modeled after
homes of some Native American
groups, provided shelter for
early settlers in New England.

or injured. Ships, airplanes, trains, buses, and auto-
mobiles stand ready to take us wherever we want to go.
In short, most Americans live quite comfortable lives.

But when the first colonists came to America, none
of these things was available to them. Their life was
very hard—almost impossible compared to life today.
Just think. These people had to build their houses with
their own hands, something many colonists had never
done before. They had to hunt and fish for their own
food, grow their own vegetables, make their clothes,
furniture, dishes, cups, bowls, spoons, and knives.

Without electricity, they got out of bed when the sun rose and retired not long after it set.

When they got sick, they had to heal themselves—and there were no medicines or clinics or hospitals as we know them today.

To travel any distances, they went by raft or boat (which they also had to build themselves) if they lived by the ocean or a river. If not, they rode a horse (if they were fortunate enough to own one) or walked. A simple trip from Boston to New York could take two weeks. Today, we can fly between those cities in less than an hour.

In short, the early colonists spent almost every hour of every day working to stay alive.

A difficult life, one hard for us to imagine? Yes, indeed. How, then, did they survive? For one, they were committed to making their settlements grow and prosper. They were not afraid of hard work. They worked together for the common good of all. And they owed a great deal to the Native Americans, who taught them many ways to prevail in what was then an alien, and very dangerous, land.

NEW ENGLAND COLONIES
Massachusetts, Connecticut,
Rhode Island, New Hampshire

MIDDLE COLONIES
New York, New Jersey,
Pennsylvania, Delaware

SOUTHERN COLONIES
Virginia, Maryland,
North Carolina, South Carolina,
Georgia

N

N H

NEW
YORK

MASS

CONN

R I

PENN

N J

MD

DEL

VIRGINIA

NORTH CAROLINA

SOUTH
CAROLINA

GEORGIA

ATLANTIC OCEAN

# CHAPTER ONE

# Colonies and Colonists

Civilization was flourishing in America long before the first English settlers arrived on its shores. That was the civilization of Native American tribes, at least 8,000 years old even then.

At the time the first settlers arrived in America, in the seventeenth century, there were nearly 400,000 Native Americans living along the east coast from what is now Canada to Georgia. Almost all belonged to one of several dozen tribes that spoke either the Algonquin or Iroquoian language. These people were mainly hunters, fishers, and gatherers, though some tribes, especially among the Iroquois, were farmers as well. Each tribe had a highly developed civilization with its own rigidly enforced laws, elected leaders, and religious beliefs.

The basic unit of all Native American societies was

the family. Next came the clan, which was made up of several related families, then the tribe, which included several clans. Algonquian tribes were formed and led by men. Iroquoian clans, on the other hand, were headed by women. All Iroquoian men, when they married, joined the wife's clan. The Iroquois were masters at organizing and running their tribes. In fact, when the founders of the United States sat down to write a constitution years later, they drew some inspiration from the way the Iroquois ran their affairs.

Still, Europeans and Native Americans had a number of differences. Chief among these was the way in which each thought of the land. The Native American never did understand the European idea of owning land. Indeed, they believed land was tribal property to be shared by everyone, because the land was the source of food, clothing, and shelter. Put another way, Native Americans were concerned with living, the Europeans with acquiring.

The English were not the first "outsiders" to explore America. Sometime around A.D. 1000, Vikings landed at various places along the Northeast coast. They even built camps, but none was permanent.

Then came other explorers—from Spain and Portugal, from France and Holland. These were followed by fishermen and traders who returned to their homes bearing colorful tales of great forests teeming with wildlife, of fish-filled waters, of rich lands, and of Native Americans eager to trade beaver pelts for cloth and tools.

Stories like these got other Europeans thinking about coming to see this new land for themselves, perhaps even settling here permanently. And so they did. Their reasons for coming were as varied as the kinds of colonies they eventually established.

First were the Spanish, who in 1565 founded the oldest city in America, St. Augustine, in what is now

Florida. The Spanish were looking for gold and gems, which they were sure littered the ground. They also came for religious reasons, and so were determined to convert the "heathen Indians" to their own religion.

After the Spanish came the first English settlers. These were a band of 140 men led by Captain John Smith, who settled Jamestown, Virginia, in May 1607. Most of Smith's band were noble-born gentlemen intent on finding gold. This group was driven to the adventure by certain English laws. At the time, there was a law that said only the eldest son could inherit his father's land and riches. Any other sons (and daughters) usually had to fend for themselves.

None of the gentlemen who sailed with Captain Smith was aware of the harsh life that lay ahead of him. Indeed, none of them had any intention of working. Like the Spanish, they expected merely to pick gold and gems off the ground, load their ship, and return to England as rich men.

But of course there was no gold for the picking, and the hard life took its toll, especially when the gentlemen refused to erect shelters or hunt and fish for their food. The result was more than half of the band of 140 men died before the first summer was over. The settlement itself would likely have failed had not more ships arrived from England in 1608. These brought 70 more settlers, including women, all determined to work to make the colony grow and prosper, which it did.

Thirteen years later, a few hundred miles north of Virginia, the second important English settlement was founded. This was the one started by the Pilgrims, who landed in Plymouth, Massachusetts, in December 1620.

There were no noble gentlemen among the Pilgrims. Rather, they were all ordinary people, many of them quite poor. Their reason for coming to America was religious persecution. In England during the early

The English settlers arrived ill-prepared
and ill-equipped to found a colony.

1600s, the government and the Church of England
were virtually the same. Anyone who argued against,
or broke, any of the laws of that church was punished
severely by the state. Any land they owned could be
taken away. They could be thrown into jail, or even put
to death—and more than a few were.

The Pilgrims, or Separatists, as they preferred to be called, separated from the Church of England because they objected to the way that church was organized and the way it demanded people should worship God. The Pilgrims wanted to do away with bishops and set prayers, altars, candles, incense, and music, for example. They wanted each church to be independent of the next and to have its ministers chosen by the people. Their service would consist only of a reading from the Bible, a sermon, and a new prayer each Sunday. Because of their beliefs, they were forced to flee England. First they went to Holland, then they organized their pilgrimage to America, where they were free to worship without interference from any government.

The Pilgrims could not have landed at a worse time, however. Winters in the Northeast are cold, harsh, and long. The land looked bleak and unfriendly. As one Pilgrim wrote, it was a "hideous and desolate wilderness, full of wilde beests and wilde men."

Of the 102 Pilgrims who landed in December 1620, only fifty lived through that first winter. The settlement appeared doomed when it was saved largely through the efforts of two Native Americans, Samoset and Squanto, both of whom spoke English. They showed the Pilgrims how to hunt, fish, and grow corn. And they introduced them to Massasoit, the great chief of the Wampanoags, with whom the Pilgrims signed a treaty that would last fifty years.

In 1624 shortly after the Pilgrims arrived, thirty Dutch families settled in Albany, in what is now upstate New York. Two years after that, another Dutch settlement was started on Manhattan Island. The Dutch called this settlement New Netherlands, a name it held for nearly forty years, until the English forced the Dutch to surrender the colony in 1664. (Looking on the east coast of America as its very own, the English did not wish to share any part of it with other nations.)

The reason the Dutch had come to America was to establish settlements so they could trade with the Native Americans and with other colonies. Because Holland was far more tolerant of differing religions than England was at the time, freedom to worship was not a strong factor for the Dutch settling in America.

Another European nation sent settlers to America at this time. This was Sweden, which, in 1638, started a settlement along the southern edge of the Delaware River in what later was to become New Jersey.

The Swedish settlers (whose country also ruled Finland at the time) included a number of Finns as well. New Sweden, as the settlement was called, was inhabited by convicts and troublemakers whom the Swedish government sent into exile with the promise they could

Massasoit, the Wampanoag chief,
and the settlers negotiated a peace.

return home when their prison terms were completed. Many did just that, but enough remained to keep the colony going. Later, New Sweden was taken over by the Dutch, who in turn lost it to the English. The Swedish and Finnish colonists, though, didn't particularly care who controlled the colony as long as they were left alone to farm and trade as they wished.

Then, in 1630, ten years after the Pilgrims landed in America, the first group of Puritan settlers established Boston, a few miles north of Plymouth. The Puritans were also seeking religious freedom, having had a number of disputes with the Church of England.

They arrived, some 100 strong, followed by another 1,000 before the year 1630 was over. These Puritan settlers were well-schooled, prosperous, and intelligent. Unfortunately, they were also bigoted. For although they left England in search of religious freedom, they were quite intolerant of anyone who refused to worship exactly as they did. Indeed, Puritans believed fervently they had a very special connection with God, and anyone who challenged their ideas was hounded out of the colony. Punishments such as public whippings or fines took care of the dissidents. For example, playing on the Sabbath, Sunday, brought a fine of more than a day's pay, whereas running, jumping, or singing on that day brought a fine nearly equal to a month's pay! Religion was something the Puritans took quite seriously. To them, it was much more than observing the Sabbath— as strict as that might be—it ruled all of life. Puritan laws were enforced every day of every week, and the church leaders and the General Court, the legislature, were in effect one and the same.

So strong was the Puritans' bigotry toward dissenters in their own ranks and toward other religions, that many of the first settlers fled Boston to start other colonies. One of these colonies was Connecticut, begun by Thomas Hooker in 1636. Another was Rhode Is-

A strict Puritan father pulls his
son home by the ear to keep
him away from village revelry.

land, founded by Roger Williams and his followers in 1638. Both men were Puritan ministers, and both were forced to flee Boston because they dared to disagree with the stern and rigid doctrine of the Puritan leaders who ran their colony with an iron fist.

The third colony was New Hampshire, settled about this time by some followers of Anne Hutchinson, a remarkable woman not only for colonial times but for any time or age. The mother of fourteen children, all born in England, she came to America when she was in her forties. She settled in Boston and soon made the Puritan leaders there angry.

Anne Hutchinson held a number of beliefs quite different from the Puritans'. For example, she believed an individual could find God's love alone, without following Puritan rules, and she held meetings in her home to talk about the sermons she had heard on the Sabbath. Eventually, she was brought to trial, convicted, and banished from the colony.

Anne Hutchinson left Boston then for Rhode Island, and afterward went to New York, where she was killed in a Native American uprising in 1643.

As news of the successes of these colonies reached England, more groups organized, got charters from the king, and came to America to start their own. These colonies included Maryland, begun by Roman Catholics, who, like the Pilgrims and Puritans, suffered from religious persecution in England; and Pennsylvania, whose Quakers began the colony as "a haven for persecuted people." Farther south were the Carolinas, begun as a business venture, and Georgia, peopled partly by settlers released from the infamous debtors' prisons of the time.

In seventeenth-century England people who owed money, whether they were scoundrels or decent people who could not raise enough money to pay off their bills, were hounded and cast into prison. There they were treated quite inhumanely, often brutally. Their only chance for freedom was to have a friend pay off their debts. To James Edward Oglethorpe, such actions were not only unfair, they robbed England of the contributions of what were, for the most part, good people. He arranged to have many of these prisoners freed if they would follow him to Georgia.

Eventually, the colonies grew to thirteen in number and then challenged and won their independence from England in the American Revolution. Those thirteen colonies were New Hampshire, Massachusetts, New York, Rhode Island, Connecticut, Pennsylvania, New Jersey, Delaware, Maryland, Virginia, North Carolina, South Carolina, and Georgia.

At the time the American Revolution began in 1775, the population of the colonies had grown from the first 140-man settlement in Virginia to more than two million people. For many of the two million, and for many of those who had preceded them to America, the great lure was more than a chance to escape religious persecution, or relief from repressive governments that taxed people unmercifully, established debtors' prisons, kept people from voting or owning land or having any say at all in how their lives would be lived. It was not even the promise of great riches. It was simply the chance to own land, which itself meant a family could be reasonably sure of enough food, shelter, and clothing—things few people in Europe had in those times.

# CHAPTER TWO

# Homes

The early settlers who braved the long and dangerous sea voyage to America realized they were leaving their old way of life behind. This did not mean, however, they simply abandoned all the old ways. For example, the kind of homes they eventually built were often near copies of those they had inhabited in Europe.

First, however, was the need for temporary shelter from the weather. In the northern colonies this often meant putting up what was called an English wigwam. English wigwams were patterned after the wigwams Algonquin Indians lived in. These were dome-shaped, semitemporary structures framed by slender tree limbs tied together, usually by reeds, and bent to form the dome. But where the Native Americans covered the framework with tree bark or animal skins, English settlers used a mixture of straw or grass mixed with mud or clay. The settlers called this "wattle and daub," and it was used by the poor in all parts of England.

An early engraving of an
Algonquin village shows
how their shelters were built.

The wigwam had only one room, sometimes as much as twenty feet across and high enough for an adult to stand up in. It was simply furnished with a crude table, a bench or two, and a chair. (The Algonquin wigwams were furnished with a raised platform that served both as seats and beds.) The first English wigwams had dirt floors but no chimneys. A hole in the roof carried the smoke from cooking and heating fires. The entrance was usually a low doorway (often only three feet high).

Iroquois Indians, who stayed put in one place longer than Algonquins, lived in large community houses, called longhouses. These were typically fifty to one hundred feet long, twenty feet wide, and twenty feet high. The framework consisted of poles set into the ground, coming to a peak in the center of the roof. The framework was covered in tree bark. An entrance was cut into one end of the longhouse, and a number of smoke holes cut into the roof served as chimneys.

Each longhouse held members of the same clan. Every family within the clan had its own room, about six by twelve feet, off a long central corridor. In front of each family room, a crude fireplace was used for cooking and heating. The family room was furnished with two levels of platforms, the lower for sitting and sleeping, the upper for storage. Opposite the entrance was a larger, common, storage room for the entire house. The number of longhouses in an Iroquoian village varied according to the number of clans. Whatever the number, the longhouses were always enclosed by a tall fence surrounding the entire village.

When the Dutch settlers founded New Netherlands, their first shelters were often dugouts. These were good-sized pits dug into the ground or the side of a hill. The hole was covered with rough-cut wooden planks.

Because settlers in the southern colonies enjoyed milder weather than those in the northern or middle colonies, their first shelters were even cruder than wigwams and dugouts. Here the lean-to was the first likely shelter. A typical lean-to was made of sturdy tree branches or wooden planks placed at an angle against a large tree or the face of a cliff.

Once the colonists gained a permanent foothold in America—and had harvested their first crops and learned from Native Americans where the hunting and fishing were best—they turned their attention to more permanent kinds of shelters. The first of these houses were almost all built of wood, a material found in abundance in every settlement. In fact, so many wooden structures were built that the seventeenth century in America became known as a period of wooden houses, wooden churches, and wooden public buildings.

In a typical wooden house of the time, a visitor entered a single room with a floor covered in wooden planks. This room often had a huge walk-in stone fireplace that took up an entire end wall. The fireplace was used for cooking and for heating the house.

Atop this "living room," wooden beams were set. These ran the full width of the house. Another set of wooden planks was then set on the beams, making a second story that was reachable by ladder. This upper space—really a loft more than a separate room—was the place where children slept.

Any windows in the house were few and narrow, letting in some light while keeping out the worst of any bad weather. Window "glass" was most often paper soaked in linseed oil. In the early years of the colonies glass windows were rare and valuable. In fact, those settlers lucky enough to have glass windows would likely remove them when they left their homes for any length of time! (Similarly, nails were rare and costly. Most houses were held together by wooden pegs. Settlers who used nails in their houses would likely burn down the house to retrieve the nails if they were moving.) These houses were often square, perhaps twenty feet on a side, with low ceilings and steeply pitched roofs.

Houses like these, which had their origin in the northern colonies, could be found in the middle and southern colonies as well. But the houses in those regions were changed to fit the mood of the inhabitants and the weather.

For example, the Dutch settlers of New Nether-

The "living room" of a typical colonial
wooden house was the center of family life.

lands made sure their houses had wide doors, the upper part of which could be opened separately. And they
included many large windows. No gloomy and dark
interiors for the Dutch settlers.

A second difference lay in the interior of the Dutch
houses. Here the kitchen was separated from the main,
or living room. The kitchen was where the Dutch enter-
tained their visitors, who came often and stayed long
hours. It was well lighted, comfortable, and always
filled with the delicious aromas of Dutch cooking.

In Dutch households, visitors
and family clustered in the kitchen,
not in the separate living room.

Yet a third difference involved beds—or what
seemed to be a lack of beds in Dutch houses. Where the
New England colonists slept in rough four-posters (the
better ones with feather mattresses, others with mattresses stuffed with woolen rags), beds in the homes of
the Dutch settlers were often concealed behind cur-
tained walls. Lift the curtain aside and there was the
bed, looking not unlike a cupboard or built-in storage
compartment.

In the southern colonies, an overhang, or "eave" supported by columns, was often added to the basic structure. This was said to give the houses the look of a fine mansion. Beyond looks, the eave was helpful in providing shade from the hot summer sun. Many southern homes had balconies extending out from the upper rooms.

Two other kinds of houses were popular in the colonies in the seventeenth century. One of these was the saltbox, found mainly in settlements in the north. The saltbox rose two stories high in front but, because of a steeply pitched back roof, only one story in the rear. The saltbox had fewer windows than square colonial houses and was simpler and less expensive to build. What is more, it could be added to easily by extending a room off the back.

The second popular house had a great influence on the history of America. This was the log cabin. This kind of housing was brought to the colonies by Swedish and Finnish settlers living in what is now New Jersey. The log cabin was the simplest, least expensive, and most quickly built form of permanent housing. As such, it was the house of choice for poorer colonists, no matter where they came from.

The typical log cabin was rectangular in shape, as long and as wide as the builder cared to make it. It had a center door and windows that varied in number and placement according to the ideas of the builder. At first, many windows were covered by leather, oiled paper, or wooden shutters. In later years glass replaced those kinds of window coverings.

As the eighteenth century began, the colonies entered a time of growth and increasing prosperity, especially after 1730. One result of this was houses became more comfortable, some even grandly elegant, and building materials other than wood came into use.

One of these new building materials was stone,

found mostly in houses in the northern colonies where there was easy access to the material. The other building material was brick. Brick kilns popped up everywhere in the colonies and soon bricks were made in such quantities that exporting them to the islands of the West Indies became a profitable business for many people.

By the middle of the eighteenth century, there were 20,000 people living in 3,000 houses in Boston. More than half the houses were wood, the rest stone or brick. Almost all the houses were two or three stories high. Even most of the city's streets were paved with stone, prompting one visitor to note his surprise, while at the

The Coffin House, built in 1686 on
Nantucket Island, is an example
of a colonial saltbox house.

same time making the comment that some of these same streets were "crooked, narrow, and disagreeable" for walking.

At the same time in New York, which had somewhat fewer people and houses than Boston, a goodly number of houses were built in the Dutch fashion, with gables facing the street. Others, as one visitor wrote in his journal, were "spacious, genteel houses, some being four and five stories high, of hewn stone, brick, and white Holland tiles, neat but not grand."

The better homes in the northern and middle colonies were built of brick or wood, sometimes of both. If built of wood, the outsides were likely covered with clapboards, which went unpainted. The roofs were steeply pitched to shed winter snows. A typical interior layout contained four rooms and a hall with a kitchen in the back, and three or four rooms on the second floor.

The rooms had wooden floors, the staircase (which replaced the earlier ladder) included a railing, and there was much carved woodwork around doorways and fireplace mantels. Interior walls were often covered by cloth or paper. All ceilings were low and the walls had glassed-in windows with shutters.

Brick houses were generally built with massive chimneys on either end of the house. The exterior walls might be as much as 13 inches thick. Here, as in wooden houses, the floors were usually bare wood, with a few mats strewn about. Any carpets could be found in the second-floor bedrooms. So common were these wood-framed and brick homes in the northern and middle colonies, their style became known as "carpenter's colonial."

By contrast, homes in the southern colonies were as unalike as those in the northern and middle colonies were similar. Here they ranged from grand plantation mansions to small square buildings, about 12 feet by 12 feet with brick chimneys, to crude log cabins with clap-

A colonial engraver created this view
of the rapidly growing city of Boston.

boards for roofing, a kind of house one traveler described as "very bad and ill-contrived."

The majority of these "very bad and ill-contrived"
houses (which were more like small cabins, actually)
could be found on the large cotton, rice, and tobacco
plantations. These served as living quarters for the
black slaves who worked as field hands. The one-room
cabins were dark and damp, often with dirt floors and
walls of crude boards, perhaps whitewashed. Slave-

holders provided very little in the way of furniture, usually not even beds, so the slaves slept on the bare floor or on piles of straw.

The most representative of the southern plantation mansions was built of brick. The central structure often had two large wings, either connected or separate. One wing held the kitchen, the other served as a carriage house. The larger plantation mansions had twenty or more rooms, each elegantly decorated and furnished.

Less pretentious than the mansion houses, more ordinary dwellings were still quite comfortable and spacious. Each had its own yard and garden, even in such populous cities as Charleston, South Carolina, and Savannah, Georgia.

These houses were most often two-story rectangular structures of wood or brick. The front likely had a balcony, and a porch ran the entire width of the back. The dining room, along with sleeping quarters, was on the second floor. Closets and fireplaces could be found in nearly every room.

Of course, in those days, there were no bathrooms, either indoors or out of doors. Most colonists set up a kind of primitive outhouse in a corner of the barn (if they had one), or a shed some distance from the main house. In the winter, when it was often unbearably cold at night, colonists used chamberpots, which they would empty during the day. Taking baths was not a common occurrence in those days either. The colonists took their attitudes toward bathing with them to America. That meant bathing rarely, perhaps once a month at best. The colonists believed in washing their faces and hands and brushing their teeth frequently. And they combed their hair "in time and season, but not too curiously," as one old book put it. But putting their entire bodies in water was something frowned upon. Indeed, at least two colonies, Pennsylvania and Vir-

Southern homes, like this eighteenth-century
residence, were often built of brick, with
balconies and shaded entrances.

ginia, actually tried to pass laws forbidding taking a bath!

Furnishings in colonial houses during the eighteenth century ranged from the magnificent in grander homes and mansions to the strictly utilitarian in the homes of less wealthy people. The grander homes and mansions featured treasures such as hand-carved mahogany furniture—chests for storing clothing and dinnerware, beds, tables, and chairs. The paneled walls held paintings, mirrors, and elaborately woven tapestries. Crystal chandeliers hanging from the ceilings gave off the light of many candles, shining on harpsichords and other musical instruments, on silver and gold eating utensils, and on cups, plates, wine bowls, and glasses of the finest construction. Even the floors were covered in "Turkey carpets," or, as we call them today, Oriental rugs.

The homes of ordinary people were quite different, to say the least. If any family was lucky enough to own a "Turkey carpet," it was used as a tablecloth, not walked on. Tables and chairs, a chest of drawers or two to supplement built-in closets for storage, and rude beds and benches were all likely home built. Favored woods for these kinds of furnishings included maple, pine, and cypress. Later in the century, when craftsmen equalled the finest furniture makers in the world, beautiful chests, tables, and beds began to appear. (One desk made about this time by a colonial furniture maker in Newport, Rhode Island, sold at auction in our own times for $12 million!)

Any mirrors in the homes of ordinary people were likely to be small and cloudy, unlike the clear gilt mirrors found in many mansions. So too clocks, which were quite rare at first, but by the middle of the century, many were being imported from Europe and a number were made in the colonies themselves. By then

advertisements like this were appearing in all the colonies:

---

*To all gentlemen and others: There is lately arrived in Boston by way of Pennsylvania a Clock maker. If any person or persons hath any occasions for new Clocks or to have old ones turned into Pendulums, or any other thing either in making or mending, they can go to the Sign of the Clock and Dial on the South Side of the Town House.*

---

Before then, however, the most common way of telling time was by a sun dial. These were set in the street, in front of the house. Marks on the door threshold or a windowsill pointed out the noon hour.

Harpsichords, carpets, silver, and paintings began to appear in elegant colonial homes.

# CHAPTER THREE

# Clothing

**W**hen the first English colonists arrived in America, the clothing they brought was ill-suited for the rugged life they faced. In fact, many people arrived with little more in the way of clothes than those they wore on their backs. One young man who came to Virginia with Captain John Smith to seek his fortune wrote his parents in England that his one suit had quickly been worn to rags. He even lacked a coat to keep out the wind and cold. Before the clothing his parents sent reached him, the man took sick and died.

The kinds of clothing Native Americans wore depended largely on the weather and climate. Regardless of the season, however, virtually every garment was made of animal skin—mostly tanned deerskin. In the summer, men generally wore only a breechclout and moccasins; women wore two-piece dresses (with the sleeves removed) and moccasins. Until they were ten years old, Native American children went nude, after which age they dressed the same way as adults.

In the winter, men would add leggings, coats, and perhaps a robe made of bear, beaver, or otter skins. Women put the sleeves back into their dresses and wore robes also.

Native Americans liked to decorate their clothing with bird feathers, beads, stones, and bits of metal. They also tattooed designs on their skin and painted their faces and arms. Women wore their hair long in one or two braids, to which they fastened shells or feathers or pieces of metal as ornaments. Warriors often shaved their heads, leaving only a "scalp lock" down the center, ending in a long braid. Other men wore their hair long and decorated it with bird feathers. Long or short, the hair was almost always rubbed in bear fat to make it shine.

In those early years of the colonies, there were no stores where people could buy their clothes—even if they had money. As a result, most people wore clothes of homespun; that is, cut from cloth spun and woven at home. One kind of cloth was linen, spun from the flax plant. A second kind was wool, woven from the soft, curly hair of sheep.

So important were these animals to life in the northern colonies that settlers in Boston and Plymouth passed laws protecting sheep. For example, sheep could not be sold to anyone outside those colonies. Each family had to provide one person to be a wool spinner. The village leaders appointed a director for every ten spinners. Each group was given a quota of wool to spin into thread, which was then woven into cloth.

Woolen cloth was often colored with natural dyes. Some tree bark yielded a yellowish- or a reddish-brown (called russet) color. The juices of certain berries provided a crimson dye, whereas the iris flower gave a delicate purple dye.

Leather tanned from the hides of wild animals (yet another skill the settlers learned from Native Americans) as well as those from cows, goats, and pigs was also used in clothing. These hides were cut into hats, jackets, shoes, and boots.

The everyday clothing settlers in the northern colonies wore was heavy and coarse. One reason for this was the long winters. The other was the staunchly religious Pilgrims and Puritans who settled those colonies. They were not "fancy" people. They did not care for elegant clothing. Indeed, they even rejected buttons as too fancy. They used strings, which they tied to keep their shirts and coats closed.

Men generally wore linen shirts and knee breeches with woolen stockings that came over the knees. A jacket, called a "doublet," which reached to the hips, was worn over the shirt. Their hats were wide brimmed and high crowned. Their shoes or boots, made of leather with double-thick soles, were ill-fitting. (Early shoes and boots were cut the same for both left and right feet.)

In warmer weather, many farmers shed their shoes and stockings and went about their chores barefoot. But in the cold winter months, they kept their shoes or boots on and added a second shirt, a doublet, and a long woolen cloak or a leather jacket as an outer garment.

Colonial women in the northern colonies wore linen blouses, too, which they tucked into long woolen skirts, and woolen stockings with shoes not unlike the men's. In addition, the women covered their skirts with a long white apron and wore a white neckcloth over a sleeveless doublet.

Some women wore brimmed hats similar to the men's, but most adopted a woolen, close-fitting cap somewhat like a bonnet. Children's clothing was similar in style to their parents', right down to the subdued colors like tans, browns, russets, and blues.

In keeping with the thrifty nature of these early

An old engraving of Puritans
walking to church shows
their traditional, sober dress.

settlers, their clothing—even boots and shoes—was made at home. The same cloth was cut and recut, sewn and resewn, and handed down from one generation to another until it was so patched and threadbare, it was useless.

Those were the everyday clothes settlers in the northern colonies were likely to wear. In addition to an everyday outfit, most family members had two more. One was known as the "second best," and although similar in style and color, was used for trips to market or for running errands in town. The best outfit, which was treasured and carefully saved, was set aside for use only on Sunday, or "Sabbath Day," as these colonists called the day set aside for religious worship.

In the northern colonies (as in all others), clothing also marked a person's social position. Thus, clothing worn by, say, a minister or judge or lawyer was more carefully made and more elegant than that worn by ordinary people. For example, a judge might wear a scarlet robe while hearing a case in court. The lawyers arguing the case were likely to be dressed in black velvet suits.

Common people were discouraged from wearing what officials called "excess clothing," however. In fact, Puritan church leaders went so far as to speak out against the "great disorder general throughout the country in costliness of apparel and following new fashions" by colonists who prospered as the colony grew in size and importance.

Clothing styles were quite different in the southern colonies, especially Virginia. There, for example, styles favored those of the Cavaliers (soldiers of the king of England) rather than the subdued dress of the Pilgrims and Puritans. Whereas most Pilgrims and Puritans cut their hair short and went without beards, the Cavaliers liked long, flowing hair and neatly trimmed beards. In time, wigs became the rage with these men.

In the southern colonies, more
elaborate costumes were favored.

They wore them in all kinds of weather, hot and cool
both. Their wigs were powdered and worn long and
curly, or were braided in a kind of ponytail called a
"queue."

The Cavaliers also favored low-crowned hats with
soft brims. The hats were often decorated with
feathers. Their shirts had wide, puffy sleeves and likely
were embroidered with flower designs. If they could
afford it, they wore silk stockings with their breeches. If

not, they settled for woolen stockings much like those worn by settlers to the north.

A cloak was the favored outer garment, or a full cut coat. The richer the man, the more elaborate and colorful was his coat.

As one might expect, clothing worn by indentured servants and slaves was often quite different from that worn by the colonists. This was especially true in the South, where field hands wore simple shirts and trousers made of homespun linen, usually dyed blue. Most of the people went barefoot. On the other hand, slaves employed as house servants wore nicer clothing, more fitting for duties such as waiting on table, or being a maid, a butler, or footman on the owner's coach. Slaves who worked in a trade (as many in the northern colonies did), such as a carpenter or printer or sailor, wore clothing similar to that worn by freemen engaging in the same kind of work.

Women in the southern colonies wore clothing similar to that worn by women in Boston and Plymouth at first. But as the southern colonies grew and prospered, the fashions for women changed. They turned to elaborate dresses with puffy sleeves that reached the elbows. The skirts billowed out as far as four feet, helped by hoops sewn into them. White or gray stockings gave way to brightly colored silk hose. And jewelry was added to the costume. Jeweled pins, earrings, and necklaces were the favored pieces.

The middle colonies were settled by two different groups of people. One was the Dutch in New Netherlands. The other group was the Quakers, who settled Pennsylvania. Just as they differed in their views of religion and other aspects of life, so they differed in their dress.

Clothing the Dutch wore tended to be colorful and as well made as the wearers could afford. They wore big hats decorated with plumes or feathers. They wore

A Dutch couple, strolling along
the canal in old Manhattan,
appear in typical Dutch attire.

Quaker men, with traditional hats
firmly in place, attend a meeting in 1682.

elaborate collars, always starched, often ruffled as well.
Their breeches were loose and floppy. Their shoes featured silver buckles. Blue, green, and yellow were the
favorite colors of the Dutch.

Dutch women wore several skirts (called petticoats)

at the same time. These were striped and short enough to show stockings decorated with embroidered designs on the ankles. The women also wore a thin girdle, or belt, around the waist. Besides being a part of the fashion of Dutch women's clothes, the girdle served another purpose as well. Dangling from it on ribbons or chains were scissors, keys, pincushions and the like, along with a decorated pouch or two for carrying extra items. A loose-fitting jacket was worn as an outer garment, and a quilted cap of linen or calico cloth completed the outfit.

Clothing like this was quite a contrast to the fashions of the Quakers. Much like the Pilgrims and Puritans, the Quakers were not showy people. Quaker men wore a long coat that fell to the knees. It was buttoned down the front. The sleeves were rolled back to show the cuffs of the shirt. Quaker men also wore knee breeches, plain stockings, and shoes. Quaker headgear was recognized throughout the colonies. The hat was wide-brimmed with a low crown. In keeping with their belief that no person was better than another, Quakers never raised their hats to anyone, not even people in authority. They also wore their hats indoors, even while eating.

In a time when children were thought of as miniature adults, it is really not surprising that their clothing was like their parents'. One of the few differences was with the clothing Dutch children wore. Instead of leather shoes with buckles, they wore wooden shoes. Otherwise, only the size of the outfits distinguished adult clothing from that made for children.

# CHAPTER FOUR

# Food

Early settlers in America may have lacked many of the things they were used to in England—houses, shops to buy clothes in, tools, for example—but one thing they did not lack was food. The bays and ocean swarmed with fish, eels, clams, and oysters. The forests teemed with deer, wild turkey, pheasants, and other game animals. The rich soil yielded bountiful crops of vegetables and fruits once the settlers learned how to farm in this new land.

All this did not happen overnight. In fact, when the Pilgrims landed at Plymouth in 1620, it was winter and well past the time to harvest any crops. The people were tired and discouraged from their stormy sixty-six day ocean crossing. And now they had to face a bitter northern winter.

And bitter it was. Nearly half the settlers died that winter. But spring brought warmth and new hopes—and friendly Native Americans who gave the gift of corn to the colonists. Corn, a food no European had seen before, soon became the staple of the diet in every colony. What is more, every part of the corn plant was put to good use.

Corn stalks fed cattle in winter. Corn husks filled the mattresses people slept on. Corn cobs were used as stoppers for jugs and handles for tools. The cobs were also carved into pipe bowls from which the colonists smoked their tobacco.

But before any of this took place, the settlers had to be taught how to farm corn. The Indians showed them when to plant the kernels ("when the leaves of the white oak tree grow as large as the ear of a mouse"). The colonists learned to put one herring (a small fish used as fertilizer) and five kernels of corn into a mound of soil. ("One for the blackbird, one for the crow, one for the cutworm, and two to grow" was the rhyme the colonists made up to explain the five kernels to a mound, or hill.)

Then, when the corn stalks were two or three feet tall, the settlers were shown how to plant squash, beans, and pumpkin seeds around the stalks. The cornstalks acted as beanpoles and shaded the squash and pumpkin vines from the hot summer sun. Later, Native Americans taught the colonists how to harvest the corn, grind it into meal, and preserve it to keep it from going bad.

Corn was central to the lives of Native Americans. They grew it along with several kinds of squash, and beans, and called those the three sisters, a trio of spirits who watched over all their food crops.

Every Native American village had its vegetable garden as well. The land for the garden was cleared by the men, but it was the women and children who planted, tended, and harvested the crops. It was the women who prepared all the meals.

To supplement the vegetables, women and children gathered nuts and wild plants from the forest, espe-

Native Americans devised a method of
pounding corn with a pestle suspended from
a tree branch. The branch acted as a spring to
raise the pounder after each down beat.

cially acorns, chestnuts, berries, onions, and ginger.
The men fished and dug oysters, clams, and mussels,
and hunted with bows and arrows for deer, wild turkey,
and other game.

Native Americans generally roasted, baked, or
boiled their food, which they might also sweeten with

maple syrup. Meals were washed down with any number of different drinks, from fresh water to tea to a kind of lemonade made from wild berries. Any food that wasn't to be eaten immediately was preserved, usually by drying or smoking.

Native Americans in the southern colonies ate most of the same kinds of food, but they added a few of their own. One was called "coontie," made from the roots of native plants. The roots were ground and pounded into flour and baked into cakes. Another food was bread made from dried persimmon fruit, and *thirs*, a cabbage-like dish made from parts of palm trees.

Naturally, the settlers did not come empty-handed to America. On the ship they ate hardtack (a kind of biscuit), salt horse (pickled meat), dried fish, and cheese. They washed down their meals with beer.

They also brought seeds that grew into onions, peas, turnips, carrots, spinach, and parsley. And they had a few sheep, chickens, and hogs, along with some horses, but no cows. The first cattle arrived from England in 1624. Soon after they established their settlements, the colonists sent back to England for apple seeds and started small orchards.

Yet through it all, corn remained the king in all the English colonies in America. Ground into meal, it was moistened with water or buttermilk and fried on a hot griddle. The result was johnnycakes, or journeycakes, as they were sometimes called, because they were often carried on long trips.

Cornmeal boiled with milk became corn mush, or hasty pudding. It was also fried as a kind of pancake called slapjacks, and served hot with a topping of molasses, maple syrup, or maple sugar. Corn was served in Indian pudding, roasted in its husk on hot embers, or steamed over hot stones in an outdoor cooking pit. Corn was even made into a kind of beer.

Virtually all the meals were prepared in the common room, or what is called the kitchen today. The common room was attached to the house in the northern and middle colonies. In the southern colonies, where summers were hot and humid, the kitchen was often a separate building, some distance from the living and sleeping quarters.

Wherever the common room was located, it was sure to have a great stone fireplace, where all the meals were cooked. These fireplaces were huge, often more than eight feet across the opening and five feet high—big enough for an adult to walk into.

Although most families had a large iron skillet for frying, and a spit or two for roasting meat, most meals were cooked in a large iron pot. These were called "spoon meats," but they were really stews of meat or fish and vegetables, perhaps spiced with salt, pepper, and ginger. One kind of "spoon meat" is still popular today. That is the New England boiled dinner. It consisted of corned beef, cabbage, and any root vegetables available at the time of cooking such as carrots, parsnips, and turnips.

The basic foods in all the colonies were quite similar. For example, corn, beans, squash, and pumpkins flourished in gardens and on farms from Massachusetts to Georgia. Fish, eels, clams, oysters, and crabs, and meats such as deer, turkey, chicken, goose, rabbit, and pork were also likely to be found on any table in the colonies.

The preferred drink was cider. This might be apple cider, pear cider (called perry), or peach cider (known as peachy). Beer was a popular drink, too. Although not many people drank fresh milk, quite a lot of it was reserved for use in making butter and cheeses. Tea, coffee, and even chocolate might also be found on the colonists' table—if they had the money to pay for these imported delicacies.

What butter or cheeses were available were usually

The colonial common
room was the scene of
many household activities.

made in the home by women and the older children.
Neither one was simple to make—they both required
time, patience, and lots of work. Here, for example, are
early instructions for making butter.

*As soon as you have Milked, Strain your Milk into a*
*Pot and stir it often for Half an Hour, then put it*
*away in your Pots or Trays. When it's Creamed, skim*

*it exceedingly Clean from the Milk, and put your
Cream into an Earthen Pot, and if you do not Churn
immediately for Butter, shift your Cream once in
twelve hours into another clean Pot. When you have
Churned, Wash your Butter in three or four Waters,
then Salt it as you will have it, and Beat it well. Let it
stand in a Wedge if it be to pot, till the next Morning,
beat it again and make your Layers the thickness of
three Fingers, and then throw a little Salt on it. And
so do until your Pot is full.*

---

Cheeses were no less time-consuming to make and
involved the addition of many more ingredients and
weeks or months of aging before they were deemed
ready to eat.

The big differences among foods in the colonies lay
in the way the foods were prepared. In Massachusetts,
for example, beans were slowly cooked for hours in an
iron pot with salt pork, onions, and molasses. The result
was the now-famous Boston baked beans.

The Dutch settlers in New Netherlands used lots of
butter in their cooking. They also made sweet dishes
like waffles, crullers, and doughnuts. And besides
hasty pudding, which the Massachusetts colonists also
enjoyed, the Dutch cooked samp porridge. This was a
kind of hasty pudding with pork or beef and vegetables
added to the coarse cornmeal-milk base. Samp porridge cooked slowly for three days before it was eaten.

Settlers in the southern colonies ate lots of hominy.
Hominy is coarsely ground hulled corn, boiled in water, and often flavored with salt and pepper, and perhaps butter as well.

Slaves on southern plantations had their own diet.
On Mondays they lined up for their weekly food ration
granted by the owners. A typical ration would include a
peck (eight quarts) of cornmeal, some molasses, and
three pounds of salt pork (something like bacon). Most

*Hare or Rabbit trussed for Roasting*

*Hare or Rabbit for Roasting or Boiling*

*A Goose*

*Breast*  *Back*

*Ducks*

THE
# FRUGAL HOUSEWIFE,
OR
## Complete Woman Cook.

WHEREIN

The Art of Dreſſing all Sorts of Viands,
with Cleanlineſs, Decency, and Elegance,

Is explained in

Five Hundred approved RECEIPTS, in

| | |
|---|---|
| Roaſting, | Paſties, |
| Boiling, | Pies, |
| Frying, | Tarts, |
| Broiling, | Cakes, |
| Gravies, | Puddings, |
| Sauces, | Syllabubs, |
| Stews, | Creams, |
| Haſhes, | Flummery, |
| Soups, | Jellies, |
| Fricaſſees, | Giams, and |
| Ragoos, | Cuſtards. |

Together with the BEST METHODS of

| | |
|---|---|
| Potting, | Drying, |
| Collaring, | Candying, |
| Preſerving. | Pickling, |

And making of ENGLISH WINES.

To which are prefixed,

Various BILLS OF FARE,

For DINNERS and SUPPERS in every Month of the Year;
and a copious INDEX to the whole.

By SUSANNAH CARTER,
Of CLERKENWELL.

LONDON.
Printed for F. NEWBERY, at the Corner of St. Paul's
Church-Yard.

BOSTON:
Re-Printed and Sold by EDES and GILL, in Queenſtreet.

1772

*The Frugal Housewife*, with illustrations
by Paul Revere, was a cookbook
published in Boston in 1772.

slaves added to this diet by cultivating small vegetable gardens.

Household servants—and slaves in the northern colonies—generally ate better food than the field hands did. Often these slaves shared the same food as their masters. It was not unknown, even, for household slaves in Massachusetts and Rhode Island to eat at the same table as their owners.

Because there was no electricity in colonial times, families generally rose at sunrise or before, and went to bed not long after dark. Upon arising, the usual custom was for everyone—including the children—to have a mug of beer. Then it was off to work in the fields for the men and older boys. The women and younger children worked in the house. Everyone had jobs to do from the time he or she was old enough to walk and talk.

Breakfast was eaten around 10 A.M. It might consist of white or corn bread, perhaps with some butter, cold meat, cider or more beer, maybe coffee or tea.

The main meal, called dinner, was eaten as late as 4:00 P.M. This would be a lavish meal of warm pork, roast beef, lamb, duck, turkey, and chicken. There likely would be fish, oysters, or clams as well, and a variety of vegetables, bread, and cider or beer. Dessert might be fruit (fresh or dried depending on the season), cheese, or pie.

When it was time to eat, the man of the house and his older sons would take their places at the table. If there was an older daughter, she would serve the food while the wife sat beside her husband. If not, the wife would serve her husband and the older sons. Any young children would stand, not sit, either at the far end of the same table or at a separate one. The younger children would eat what they were given and not speak throughout the entire meal. They also were expected to observe strict table manners. These included the following rules:

*Bite not thy bread, but break it.*
*Take not salt with a greasy knife.*
*When helping your superior to an article he shall ask*
*for, throw it not at him.*

The food was usually brought to the table in wooden bowls. It was then ladeled into wooden trenchers that served as plates. The trenchers were rectangular slabs of wood with the center hollowed out. One trencher served two people.

Everyone ate with his or her fingers. (There were few forks during the early years of colonial times. If a family was fortunate enough to have any, the forks were saved for special occasions.) Diners wiped their fingers on linen napkins (often after dipping them into bowls of water set on the table). If the food was too soupy to eat with the fingers, a spoon might be used, or the diners would sop up the food with chunks of bread.

If the meat or fish had to be cut into smaller pieces, the man or one of his sons would use a sheath knife. They wore these knives on their belts, and used them for general work as well as for cutting food.

Every meal was started by a blessing given by the man of the family, and the evening meal, or supper, was not begun until the children recited their ABCs and a summary of the Bible lesson they learned that day.

Once the meal was over, the serving person passed around a basket called a voider. Everything anyone ate with, including the linen napkins, was placed in the basket and taken away to be washed by the women and girls before the next meal was served.

Most of the recipes colonial women used in preparing foods were the result of long periods of trial and error. Most were not written down, but were passed from mother to daughter. In fact, the first cookbook that featured American foods like johnnycake and hasty pudding was not printed until 1796.

Nonetheless, individual recipes from colonial times have come down to us thanks to diaries, journals, and letters. Here are three such recipes.

### Peas Porridge

*Take a Quart of Green Peas, put them to a Quart of Water, a Bundle of dried Mint and a little Fat; boil till tender, then put in some beaten Pepper a piece of Butter rolled in Flour. Stir it, let it Boil, then add two Quarts of Milk, boil, take out the Mint, and serve up.*

### Pilgrim Cake

*Rub two Spoonfuls of Butter into a Quart of Flour, and wet it to Dough with cold Water. Rake open a Place in the hottest part of the Hearth, roll out the Dough into a Cake an Inch thick, flour it well on both Sides and lay it on the hot Ashes, cover it with hot Ashes and then with Coals. When cooked wipe off the Ashes and it will be sweet and good.*

### Hasty Pudding

*Bring a container of water and some salt to a boil in a heavy saucepan. Slowly pour in some yellow corn-meal, stirring all the while till the mix becomes thick enough so a spoon will stand up in it. Ladle the pudding into four small bowls. Drop some butter onto each portion, then sprinkle on ground nutmeg and some molasses. Serve hot.*

# Work

The first settlers in America had to make almost everything they used with their own hands and a few simple tools. They built their houses, their furniture, the very utensils they ate with. They got the food they ate by hunting, fishing, and farming, and by tending flocks of sheep and chickens and other animals.

These hardy people wove the cloth that was cut and sewn into the clothes they wore. They made the brooms they swept up with and the buckets they carried water in. In short, except for a few items like salt, the early settlers were completely self-reliant.

Later on, as the colonies grew and prospered, many of the wealthier people began sending abroad for silks and spices, fine furniture, and silverware. They bought bricks to build houses and chimneys, and candles to light their houses.

Yet a surprising number of settlers, especially in the northern colonies, preferred the older ways. They were used to supplying their own needs and saw no reason to change. So, although villages and towns grew into major cities as more and more people came to America, the family farm or plantation remained the backbone of life right up to the end of the colonial era.

In general, life on a farm was considered better than life in a city. As cities like Boston, New York, and Philadelphia grew, the seamy sides of life found in any large city began to appear. Bad housing, crime, poor (or nonexistent) sewage systems, and badly run jails where inmates were routinely beaten and poorly fed were common. So was terrible treatment of the poor and mentally ill. The former were often treated like criminals, the latter regularly whipped in public and then driven out of town. Even the religious leaders did little to ease life for the less fortunate. Whatever misfortunes fell upon a family were considered "God's punishment."

Despite all this, life on a farm was not easy either.

From the first cry of the rooster welcoming the faint gray streaks of dawn to the dusk of evening, the farm was a beehive of activity in which everyone had work to do. Indeed, there was so much work that many farms relied on outside help. Any outside help, however, was not hired hands; it was indentured servants or slaves.

Not everyone who came to America in the early years was able to pay the cost of the voyage. Some people—often entire families—signed contracts with people who paid for the passage. These contracts indentured, or bound, the person (or persons) to work off the cost by laboring for three, five, or even ten years to the one they were indebted to. After their term of labor was up, indentured servants were free to go where they wished. Some were even given a small sum of money to help them buy land of their own.

During the time of their service, indentured servants—whether adults or children—were owned by their master. As one notice of the times explained, "a

The colonial farm family worked
together at harvesttime.

servant's time belongs to his master." Indentured servants could be worked, punished, fed, or taken into the master's family at the whim of the master. If, on the voyage to America, a man died at sea (which many did), his widow was assessed the debt for his passage as well as her own. Any children were bound to servitude until they reached the age of eighteen or twenty-one, and families were often separated as masters sold their servants to other owners.

In short, indentured servants were really no more than slaves, with one exception. The exception was that these servants gained their freedom once they worked off their contracts. (But even that was not the case with all indentured servants. Many found themselves so poor—in health as well as in material things—their only hope of survival was to sell themselves for another term of servitude.)

Unlike indentured servants, slaves were the property of their masters for their entire lives. From the time the first group of slaves reached Virginia in 1619 on a Dutch vessel, they were eagerly sought after by plantation owners in that colony and in the Carolinas and Georgia as well.

The larger plantations in the southern colonies had upwards of one hundred slaves—men, women, and children—most of whom worked as field hands tending to the cotton, rice, or tobacco crops. They worked under overseers, usually white men, who demanded absolute obedience under threats of whippings. The hours of work were long—often from dawn till dusk six days a week, with Sundays and holidays off. The days were hot and the work very hard. These people got no money for their services.

Slaves had few, if any, personal freedoms and were slaves for life, unless the owner chose to free them. Any children born to slaves belonged to the owner and were bought and sold like any other ordinary property. The

Southern plantations prospered through
the labor of large numbers of enslaved people.

result was that many slave families were broken up. For
example, a husband might have to stay with the owner
while his wife and perhaps some of their children were
sold to other owners.

Most plantation owners put twenty or so slaves to
work in the main house as butlers, maids, cooks, and so

on. A very few were trained in carpentry, barrel making, and other skills necessary to running such a large business as a plantation.

The slave trade was not limited to the southern colonies. After a visit to Boston in 1687, a French traveler wrote home, "You may also here own Negroes and Negresses, there is not a house in Boston however small may be its means, that has not one or two."

That was to be expected, for the New England colonies, and especially Boston and Newport, Rhode Island, became the center of the slave industry in the 1700s. It started with the "Triangle Trade." Ships engaged in this kind of trade carried rum from Massachusetts and Rhode Island ports to Africa, where they traded the cargo for slaves. The slaves were then shipped to the West Indies for sugar and molasses. The "triangle" was completed when the sugar and molasses (along with some slaves as well) were shipped back to the colonies, where rum was made from the cargo and the whole process started again.

The Triangle Trade was immensely profitable for ship owners. The rum cost 25¢ a gallon to make. It took about 200 gallons of rum (worth about $50) to buy a slave, who could then be sold in the West Indies, or the colonies, for up to $400.

Slaves could be found in every northern colony, but never in the numbers found in the South, where they were crucial to running the large plantations. In the mid 1700s, for example, about one in fifty persons in the northern colonies was a slave. In the Carolinas, by way of contrast, two of every three persons were slaves. Because there were no large plantations in the northern colonies (the soil and weather conditions were not conducive to large farms), most slaves there worked as house servants or were trained in any one of a number of trades. Slaves were bakers, carpenters, tailors, printers, blacksmiths, and so on. A few ran the businesses of their owners, and some even apprenticed to doctors and eventually started their own medical practices.

Despite this, these people were still slaves, which meant they lived under separate laws called slave codes. The codes would not allow blacks to marry whites, to

On colonial farms, the men, women, and children all had work-filled days. Even candles were made at home.

ride ferries (for fear they would run away), to leave the colony they lived in, or to be on the streets after nine o'clock in the evening.

Ordinarily, slaves in the northern colonies lived in the owner's house, in a separate room. They were allowed to marry other slaves (or free blacks, or Native Americans) but any children would belong to the slave owner. If the husband and wife were owned by different masters, any children became the property of the wife's owner. And although selling slaves and breaking up families was not as frequently done as in the southern colonies, it did happen.

Eventually, people in the northern colonies were persuaded that slavery was an evil. By the late 1700s, every one of those colonies abolished the practice. Sadly, slavery was to continue in the southern colonies for more than half a century after that.

Besides blacks captured or bought in the West Indies and Africa, the colonists often enslaved Native Americans who were taken prisoner in the several wars that broke out in the colonies from time to time. A number of these Native Americans were forced to work as house servants or field hands. Others were shipped to Europe where they were sold as common property.

After washing up outdoors in cold water with homemade soap (remember, colonial homes had no bathrooms), the father and his older sons, along with any male servants, milked the cows and put them out to pasture. At the same time, the mother, daughters, and any children too young to work in the fields busied themselves with preparing the day's meals. This meant hauling water from a nearby river or pond, collecting eggs from any hens, building the fire in the great stone fireplace, taking out the bread that had been slowly cooking all night, and setting food on the table.

After breakfast the real work began. While the women and younger children cleared the table, the men and older boys headed back out to the fields. If their work was to take them far from the house, they might pack a meal of johnnycakes, cheese, and cider. But more likely, they would be back in the house for dinner, the main meal of the day, about 3:00 or 4:00 P.M.

For the men, the work could be tending to the crops. It could include cutting firewood, dressing any animals they had shot while hunting, butchering a pig or dressing a few chickens, seeing to the smokehouse where meats were being preserved, and so on.

Meanwhile, the youngest children were sent to tend the kitchen garden, a fixture on any colonial farm or plantation. The garden would likely have peas, onions, turnips, carrots, and other vegetables growing, and spices like thyme, parsley, and marjoram.

It would also likely have a flower bed or two. There were plants like chamomile, a daisy look-alike; madder, a plant whose yellow flowers held berries used both in dying cloth and as a medicine; and hops, whose flowers were used in brewing beer. A strawberry patch, some fruit trees, and, in the southern colonies, a few nut trees, might also be part of the kitchen garden.

Although the men killed the animals (saving the hides for tanning into leather), it was the women who cut the meat into chops and roasts and steaks, and who prepared it for preserving in the absence of refrigeration. Some meats would be pickled, some dried, and some smoked.

Without electricity, the colonists had to make their own kinds of lighting devices. The kitchen fireplace provided some light (along with heat), but this was never enough.

One way to add light was with a "candle set," a torch made of the limbs of pitch pine trees. These would be stuck into the fireplace hearth—and would give off as much smoke as light.

Every other means of lighting was based on burning either wax or fat, a way of providing light that even then was more than three thousand years old.

One way of lighting with fat, or grease, was the rush lamp. Here a length of rush, a kind of grasslike reed, was soaked in cooking grease and then ignited. A second was the "betty lamp," an iron dish filled with grease into which a linen wick was placed. Neither of these was very efficient, for they had to be watched carefully or they would go out. Worse, they smoked and gave off a horrible smell as they burned.

Then came candles, a great improvement. The first candles were made of tallow, fat from sheep or cattle. Candle-making was a job for women and younger children. It involved melting chunks of fat in an iron kettle hung in the fireplace.

While the fat (which women had been saving for months) was melting, the children tied wick strings onto a thin stick, as many as eight strings on each. When the fat was melted, the older women took the wick strings and dipped them into the hot tallow. These were then placed on a hanging rack until the tallow cooled and hardened. This was repeated over and over again until the candles were the right size and thickness. Although tallow candles burned longer and gave off more light than rush or betty lamps, they still smoked and gave off a bad smell.

Then the colonists discovered bayberry candles. The bayberry bush grows all along the Atlantic coast of America. In the fall it produces a grayish white, waxy berry. Children gathered the berries, which were then boiled in water. As the berries boiled, the wax in them floated to the surface and was skimmed off. It was allowed to harden and was remelted when making candles. Bayberry candles burned clean and gave off a very pleasant aroma. In fact, so prized were bayberry candles that in time people began making them for export to England.

By then, candle molds had come into use. These let women make twenty or more candles at one time merely by pouring hot wax into molds which had wicks already inserted. Candle molds eased this time-consuming task for colonial women and children.

That did not mean, however, that their days were any easier. For the colonists made all the soap they washed with. Like candles, a basic ingredient of soap was animal fat. Another was lye. Lye was made by pouring boiling water over a mix of wood ashes (saved from fires) and straw. As the boiling water seeped through the ashes and straw, it turned into a tea-colored liquid called lye. The lye was collected in wooden boxes or barrels until there was enough to use in making soap. Collecting enough lye could mean boiling water and pouring it through ashes and straw for a week or more.

Once there was enough lye, the women placed a huge iron kettle outside the house and started a fire under it. The lye and animal fat were dumped into the kettle and stirred constantly until the mixture turned into a kind of soft soap. Of course, at the same time, the soap makers had to be sure to keep the fire blazing.

Whatever soap the mixture yielded was stored in special crocks. Because it was such a hard task, most colonial women made soap only once a year, in the spring. Sometimes they added salt to the lye and fat mixture. Doing this would result in a harder, longer-lasting soap, for better cleaning. But since salt was so expensive and was one item all the colonists had to buy, not everyone could afford to use it in making soap. Finally, with salt added or not, the soap used in colonial days was far less efficient, and comfortable, than soaps used today. Lye soap was quite hard on the skin and did not dissolve into suds as readily as modern soaps.

Nearly all the clothing the early settlers wore was cut from linen, wool, or leather. Again, the colonists made their own. And they washed their clothes about as often as they bathed themselves. If the colonists had a regular "wash day" for clothes, it was usually held once a month. On occasion, though, the one month stretched into two. One reason for this was that washing clothes was no easy task. It involved either hauling the clothes to a stream or pond, where they were scrubbed and pounded with rocks and perhaps some homemade soap, or hauling the water bucket-by-bucket to a large iron pot outside the house, where the clothing was soaked and hung out to dry. A second, perhaps more important, reason for not washing clothes more regularly was that the people were simply following habits formed in their native Europe, where personal cleanliness was not considered important. In fact, some Europeans believed dirt kept out sickness; others felt it somehow showed one's belief in God.

Linen comes from the flax plant. First, the plants were harvested, usually in August. They were laid out to dry in the sun, then the seed pods were pulled off. Next, the stalks were bound into bundles and soaked in a stream or a pond for several days. Then the fibers were taken from the plant, carefully combed, and spun into thread on a spinning wheel. Finally, the thread was woven into cloth for shirts and blouses, aprons, table napkins, and so on.

Making cloth of wool was no easier. First, the sheep had to be sheared each spring. This was a job for the men and older boys. Then the wool was combed, washed, and rubbed with grease. After that, it was stroked to make it fluffy and spun into thread on a spinning wheel. Finally, it was dyed and woven into cloth on a loom.

Even the children took part in this kind of work. All children, boys and girls alike, were taught to sew, knit, and weave before they were ten years old. That way, they could help make their own clothes.

A lesson on the spinning wheel

"Bees" of different kinds were popular
social activities. An old woodcut shows
a spinning bee in a Boston park.

If all that sounds like hard work, it was. And if it
sounds as if the colonists did not have much time left
over for play, that too is true. So what they did was think
up ways of making fun of the work they did.

One thing they liked to do was organize bees.
These "bees" had nothing to do with the insect, rather

they were a gathering of people for a particular purpose. Colonists held husking bees at harvest time. These were contests to see who could husk the most ears of corn in a given amount of time. Women often held quilting bees. These involved getting a group together to sew a quilt, a bed cover, while they caught up on the news of the day.

A house-raising was another way to lighten the task of work. The men would build the frame of a house on the ground, then invite their neighbors to help them raise the frame into place so the house could be built. After the house-raising, everyone sat down to a grand Thanksgiving-like feast that could last a day or more.

Then there was feather stripping, an event that always took place in winter. Feather stripping was a contest to see who could strip the most down off goose feathers. The down was then used to stuff mattresses and pillows.

Finally, there was sugaring off time, an early spring event held in the northern and middle colonies. When the sap began to run in the maple trees (in February or March), the colonists collected it in buckets. The sap was then boiled down into maple syrup. Meanwhile, some of it was poured onto the snow, where it quickly hardened to become a delicious candy.

All this demonstrates what life was like on a colonial farm. And for many years, the family farm was the backbone of all the colonies. But as the colonies grew, settlements became villages, then towns, and finally bustling cities, where life was quite a bit different from life on the family farm.

Most of the important cities sprang up first in the Northeast, especially in New England, where the rock-infested soil made farming an almost impossible task. Settlements like Boston, Portsmouth, New Hampshire, and Bristol and Newport, Rhode Island, turned to the sea to make a living. With the men sailing off to the far corners of the world, trading lumber, horses, and other goods; or participating in the infamous Triangle Trade; or fishing, whaling, or building ships, someone had to provide the things the earliest settlers made for themselves. Trades and crafts began to flourish as the cities grew. Blacksmiths tended to horses, tinkers made

An engraving from 1770 records
the variety of trades in
the growing city of Boston.

and repaired pots and pans, furniture makers turned out cabinets and beds and other household furnishings. Factories that made bricks, nails, and bullets (as well as muskets) appeared, then tailors who made clothes, barbers who both cut hair and acted as doctors of medicine, printers who published newspapers and books, and innkeepers who opened taverns, grew in number. Glassmakers, shoemakers, and assorted other trades and crafts followed, until virtually anything needed to live could be bought instead of made or grown at home.

As cities grew, municipal buildings were put up and streets laid out and often paved with cobblestones. Churches, jails, schools, and shops opened.

Most people still walked the streets or rode horses, but the wealthier ones were carried about in sedan chairs mounted on long, sturdy poles and carried by slaves—blacks or Indians. Ferries, often no more than a man with a rowboat, would obligingly row a person across a river for a penny.

With all this growth came the usual problems of cities. There was crime and crowding, noise and pollution, and disease—especially disease in cities where sanitation facilities were nonexistent for years. At the same time, cities were exciting places, places where fortunes could be made, careers assured, adventure discovered.

# CHAPTER SIX

# School

**O**f all the groups who settled America during the colonial era, the Puritans of Massachusetts Bay Colony were the ones most concerned with schools. One important reason for this was their belief that everyone should seek the word of God in the Bible. In order to do that, of course, one had to learn how to read. To that end, the Puritans set up the first formal school in the colonies in 1635. That was the Roxbury Latin School. Four years later, in 1639, they opened the first college—Harvard—in Cambridge, just across the Charles River from Boston. These schools, however, were special schools for special students. Many colonists never had a chance—nor any wish—to attend either school. What is more, neither the Latin School nor Harvard College would take women as students.

The ordinary colonial youngster, boy or girl, from ages six to eight, might go to something called a "Dame School" for two years. The teacher in a Dame School would be a woman, most likely one whose husband had

An old engraving presents a
whimsical view of a Dame School.

died, and the classes would be held in her house. There
the children learned the alphabet, the basics of reading, some prayers, how to "cypher," that is, do simple
sums in arithmetic, and, if they were lucky, how to
write. But, although learning to read was considered
important in the early years of the colonies, learning to
write was not. In fact, well into the eighteenth century,
many people—especially women—still could not even
write their own names, though they could read the
Bible, other books, and newspapers passably well.
(Women in all the colonies had few of the freedoms
they enjoy today. This was especially true in Puritan
Massachusetts, where females were kept in check. For

example, wearing a veil or curling one's hair or gossiping brought quick punishment. A woman was even forbidden to talk about religion with her husband "lest she influence men through her emotionalism." In fact, in any venture beyond running the family farm or the household, women were hardly better off than servants and, in some families, slaves.)

The only aid to learning in the Dame Schools was a hornbook, which was not really a book at all. It was a page of writing, usually the alphabet on one side and the Lord's Prayer on the other, fastened to a wooden frame. The page of writing was covered with a sheet of animal horn thin enough to read through.

Any lessons were likely given in rhyme as a way to help the pupils remember. Some of the early lessons have come down to us, such as

---

*Thirty days hath November,*
*April, June, and September.*
*February hath twenty-eight alone,*
*And all the rest have thirty-one.*

---

The teacher, or dame, would recite these rhymes to her pupils, who would chant them back over and over again until they were committed to memory. This was called rote learning. As she taught, the dame would tend to other chores, such as spinning thread, weaving cloth, or preparing a meal.

For many colonial children, two years in a Dame School was the only formal education they received. Whatever else they learned was taught at home or by reading on their own once books became available. This was especially true of girls.

In those days, educating girls was thought to be a waste of time and money. After all, the thinking of the time went, the female's role in life was keeping house, bearing children, keeping money accounts for the family, and going to church. Indeed, John Winthrop, a governor of the Puritan settlement in Boston, was of the belief that educating girls would lead them to insanity!

In a few towns in the northern colonies, another level of school beyond Dame School was offered. This was the so-called common school. These would take students for three or four years. Not every town had a common school, however. Many towns decided they did not want to spend the money to run one. Then the government stepped in.

In 1647, the general court of Massachusetts ordered that every town of fifty or more families "appoint one within their towne to teach all such children as report to him to write and reade, whose wages shall be paid either by parents or masters of such children, or by the inhabitants in general." Failure to comply with this law resulted in a $25 fine. That was a large amount of money in those days.

The common school was most often a one-room building, dark and shabby on the inside. The only source of heat was a fireplace, and the students were required to bring firewood to school every day. Those who forgot were forced to sit as far as possible from the warmth of the fire.

As in the Dame Schools, there were no blackboards, maps, or other teaching aids. Except for the Bible, and perhaps any books the schoolmaster owned, there were no textbooks, either. In fact, it was not until 1690 that the *New England Primer* was printed, a book that became the standard school text for more than one hundred years. Because paper was hard to get, and expensive, students in common schools used birch bark. They wrote on this with lumps of lead or with goosequill pens dipped in homemade ink. Most lessons centered on the Bible. Occasionally, stories like Aesop's

The busy scene inside a one-room common school

Fables might be recited as well. Spelling, writing, and
simple arithmetic were the other principal subjects
taught.

Classes began as early as seven each morning and
ended with a prayer, around four or five o'clock in the

afternoon. School was in session six days a week, from Monday through Saturday.

The students sat on backless wooden benches arranged in rows facing the teacher. Discipline, when needed, was swift and harsh. Talking out of turn often meant a whipping with a birch rod. More serious offenses could find the student tied to the town's whipping post, where he would be lashed in public or set in the town's stocks for hours at a time.

Nor were these the only forms of discipline. Students who failed their lessons had to wear a cone-shaped dunce cap and a sign around the neck that read "Baby Good-for-Nothing." Those caught daydreaming wore a sign that read "Idle Boy." Even fingernail biters had their own form of punishment—a "Bitefinger Baby" sign.

Teachers, it seemed, did not fare much better. The pay was very low and, as often as not, given in food and a room in the home of one of the students instead of money. In many towns, the schoolmaster was required to do extra work, helping the minister of the church. The work could include leading the choir singing during Sabbath services, ringing the church bells, or digging graves in the town cemetery.

When a young girl finished, or left, the common school, she went back home to take her place in helping run the household. Boys had more choices.

Boys could go back home to help work the family farm. They could join their father in a trade, if he had one, such as barrel-making or bricklaying. If their father did not practice a trade, they could become apprentices to a tradesman and learn the skills that way. An apprenticeship meant the young boy was sent off to work (and often live) with a skilled worker. The length of the apprenticeship varied, but could last as long as seven years. During this time, the boy did all the menial tasks of the trade while he worked side-by-side with the craftsman. He might also read about the skill along

Franklin at the Press

Apprentices learned a trade by working for a craftsman. In this picture the young apprentice is Benjamin Franklin, learning to become a printer.

with his on-the-job training. At the end of the apprenticeship, the boy was deemed ready to go out on his own. Apprenticeships were often free, but sometimes the tradesman charged a fee.

Boys had one final option after completing the common school. They might go on to what was called a Latin School. The same law that ordered towns of fifty or more families to set up a common school had a second part to it. The second part ordered that towns with more than one hundred families set up a Latin School. Here the students, all boys, were prepared for college until they were about fifteen years old.

In those days that meant spending much of their school day learning to read, write, and even talk in the ancient Latin tongue. Of the few boys who went to a Latin School, fewer yet went on to college. At first the colleges trained only ministers. Later, law and medicine were added to the subjects. Still later, English, mathematics, and science became part of the expanding curriculum.

The common school system that got its start in the Massachusetts Bay Colony might seem hopelessly harsh, even cruel, by today's standards. It should be remembered, though, that for the first time in history, free schooling was made available to children of almost any background. It should also be remembered that those first common and Latin schools laid the groundwork for what was to become the American public school system.

Although none of the other colonies equalled the Puritans in their zeal for education, they did not ignore schooling either. The middle colonies—New York, New Jersey, Pennsylvania, Delaware, and Maryland—also set up schools. And, in fact, it was Pennsylvania that began the first medical school in America. Schools in the middle colonies were not free, but they did teach more practical subjects such as bookkeeping and surveying along with Bible studies and reading, writing, and arithmetic.

In the northern and middle colonies, selected slaves might be taught the basics of reading, writing, and cyphering, but usually only if their work required such skills.

If any colonies lagged in educating their children, it was the southern ones. Indeed, years after schools in the northern and middle colonies were flourishing, the governor of Virginia was arguing, "I thank God there are no free schools nor printing, and I hope we shall not have any these hundred years ... for learning has brought disobedience."

The main reason for the lack of public schools in the southern colonies was that the wealthy planters did not want ordinary people or slaves to be educated. Doing so would end a source of inexpensive labor. A second reason was that most of the communities in the South were small and scattered, so it was difficult to find enough students to begin a school.

Some communities started what were called "Old Field Schools," however. These were one-room schools built in abandoned tobacco fields. The teachers were most often unemployed ministers, and any student had to pay a fee to attend.

George Washington got most of his formal education in an Old Field School. He rode a horse ten miles each way to his school for a year, and later rowed morning and night across a river to a school in Fredericksburg, Virginia. Washington's formal education ended when he was thirteen, but his eagerness to learn kept him reading the rest of his life.

Wealthy planters and landowners did want their own sons and daughters to be educated, though. To that end, they often hired private tutors or appointed a servant to be teacher. Classes were held in a room of the main house, or in a separate building on the property, and might include the children of other planters as well.

Girls took part in basic education—reading, writing, and cyphering—but soon after that, their education shifted from academics to the social graces. They learned how to dance, play a musical instrument, draw and paint, and do needlework. Some few girls even studied English and French.

For their advanced education, the sons of wealthy southern planters were sent to England. This may help explain why, of the nine colleges founded in the colonies before the American Revolution began, only one was located in the South. That was William and Mary College, founded in Virginia in 1693, fifty-four years after Harvard College in Massachusetts accepted its first students.

# CHAPTER SEVEN

# Getting the News

In the early years of the colonies, people in one settlement had little communication with those in other settlements. That could mean not knowing what was going on in a community just a few miles away as well as what was happening in England. For example, King James I of England died in 1625. But the Pilgrims in Plymouth did not hear of his death for nearly a year, and only then because a ship from England touched shore at the colony.

For years the principal source of news in any colony was travelers. These might be trappers trading beaver pelts, peddlers selling kettles or other utensils, or simply wanderers. These people would tell the news of, for instance, a bad storm in Naumkeag (now Salem) in a remote part of Massachusetts to the settlers in Boston, or news of a spreading sickness in Sankikan (now Trenton) in New Jersey to settlers in New Amsterdam (now New York).

The roads these lone travelers followed were little more than trails Native Americans had blazed over the years. They were narrow, winding, often unmarked, and hardly wide enough for a person on foot or horseback to maneuver. Taking a horse-or oxen-pulled cart along these trails was impossible. To make things worse, there were no inns or restaurants or places to rest overnight. That meant land travel was difficult, a fact that kept many colonists close to home. Besides, the new settlers had enough to do working their own farms to be wondering about what some neighbor was doing or thinking.

Still, people did travel overland on these trails. And when they did, it usually meant walking or engaging in what was called "Walk and Ride." Walk and Ride was a way of traveling used when two people shared a single horse. It worked in the following way. One traveler would walk while the other rode the horse ahead. The rider would then tie the horse to a convenient tree, get off, and begin walking. Now the horse got a chance to rest. When the second traveler caught up, he mounted the horse and rode on ahead of the other traveler. Then *he* would dismount, tie up the horse, and start walking. This leapfrog kind of movement continued until the travelers reached their destination.

The first roads in the colonies were called "mast roads." These were roads cut deep into the forests to haul out trees that had been cut for shipbuilding. Mast roads were wide, straight, and well built, so they were easy to travel on. The problem was that mast roads seldom went where people wanted to go. People wanted roads that ran from one village to another, or from outlying farms to a town or city.

That need led to township roads, roads that went where the people wanted to go. They were wide enough to admit carts and were reasonably well built. Nevertheless, they were muddy when it rained, dusty in hot, dry weather, and covered with snow and ice in the colder months.

The biggest problem with township roads was they

had to cross private lands. Landowners who didn't like the idea of a road crossing over a particular part of their property might erect a series of gates, or simply reroute the road in some other direction. As a result, township roads tended to meander, which made traveling on them slow.

As the years passed, the road system in the colonies improved greatly. One reason for this was people wanted to trade more with other colonies and with England. And increased trade meant new and better ways to haul goods. One of these new ways was the Conestoga wagon, developed by German settlers in Pennsylvania, who relied on these large, canvas-covered wagons to carry farm goods long distances. A second new kind of transportation was a two-wheeled, horse-drawn cart used for local travel for one or two people. This was the famous "wonderful one-hoss shay" of early American poetry. A third kind of passenger vehicle was the so-called pleasure wagon, really a four-wheeled cargo cart. It was sturdy and roomy, if a bit uncomfortable to ride on (it lacked good springs to soften the ride).

Finally, there was the stagecoach, drawn by four or more horses. The stagecoach was a large wagon in which the passengers sat inside while the drivers and luggage rode outside. Stagecoaches were often over-crowded and stuffy, and their passengers were called on to help push them up steep hills or free them from deep mud.

With the advent of overland travel, inns began to spring up at strategic places along major routes of travel, usually where one road crossed another, or in a town. These early inns were places where weary travelers could spend a few hours or overnight resting up before taking on the next leg of their journey. The first of these rest stops offered bad food and not much more than a pile of hay to sleep on. But as travel increased,

Two colonial forms of transportation—the
stagecoach and a Conestoga wagon—arrive
at a country inn.

inns became larger and more comfortable and every
town had at least one.

Despite the growth of overland travel, by far the
most favored way to get from one place to another was
by water routes. Small boats, rafts, and ferries were
relatively comfortable and fast. Longer water trips were
usually taken in a vessel called a shallop. Shallops came

in many sizes, from smaller boats propelled by oars and a short sail to two-masted vessels that could carry many passengers along with cargo. One feature that set all shallops apart from other boats and ships was they could be sailed in very shallow waters, so they were equally useful in bays, rivers, and the ocean.

Whatever method of traveling was used, overland or on water, no trip was easy. Once when Governor William Bradford of Plymouth went to talk with Governor John Wintrop of Boston, the thirty-five-mile trip—largely on foot—took two days and involved "wading through swamps and crossing rivers on the back of an Indian guide" as Governor Bradford described it. Indeed, a simple fifty-mile sailing trip from Saybrook, at the mouth of the Connecticut River, to the capital city of Hartford, would take at least two days—if the winds were favorable. If not, it would take a week or more. Travelers walking between Boston or Cambridge to Hartford ordinarily spent two weeks covering the hundred-mile distance. But walking great distances was a common event in colonial days. There was a baker in Portsmouth, New Hampshire, who regularly walked sixty-six miles in one day to buy flour for his shop. He would arrange to have the flour shipped by boat, then he would stay overnight at an inn and walk the sixty-six miles back the next day. The baker continued to do this until he was eighty years old!

Travel by slaves was not allowed. Owners were afraid the slaves would run away if given the chance. As a result, most colonies passed harsh laws against such travel. For example, slaves were not permitted to leave the colony in which they lived. They were forbidden to ride ferries (the usual method of crossing rivers and bays). Any slave from New York found more than forty miles from home could be put to death. In Virginia, slaves who wandered (or ran) away from their masters might have their feet or hands cut off.

Getting the news in the colonies eventually involved more than listening to travelers talk. Every village had its town crier, who paraded through the streets ringing a bell and shouting out whatever news he had, from the time of day (or night) to the notice of a ship sailing for England in a week.

The first printing press came to the colonies in 1638 from England. But it was not until 1690 that the first newspaper was published. That was *Publick Occurrences*, which lasted only one issue before the royal governor of Massachusetts ordered it to stop printing. (He objected to the articles in the paper, which he felt might lead to challenging his authority.)

In 1704 the *Boston News Letter* was launched. This was the first regularly published newspaper in the colonies. From then on, more newspapers started up, so that by the end of the colonial era in 1775, there were well over 100 newspapers spread through all the colonies, from New Hampshire to Georgia.

In fact, by the end of the seventeenth century, an English traveler was moved to write that "the newspapers of Massachusetts, Connecticut, Pennsylvania, and Maryland are unequalled, whether with respect to wit and humor, entertainment or instruction. Every capital town on the continent prints a weekly paper, and several of them have one or more daily papers."

If newspapers were very important in helping the colonies grow and eventually free themselves from English rule—and they were—books were not. In fact, book publishing was not an important business until well into the eighteenth century. One reason was the scarcity of type. Most printers had only one or two fonts, or sets of type, so it was not really possible for them to set hundreds of pages of type at one time. Indeed, type was set letter by letter, line by line, and printed page by page.

A second reason for the lack of books was the scar-

Along with the other news of
the day, this colonial town crier
spreads the word of a lost child.

city of paper. For many years printers in the colonies
imported their paper from Europe. Doing so was
costly; moreover, imported paper was taxed by the Brit-
ish. The first papermill in the colonies started up in
Pennsylvania in 1690, but Virginia, for example, did
not have a mill until 1744, fifty-four years later.

Finally, because printing books was so costly, what

books were printed were largely "safe" books, those certain not to include revolutionary ideas that might offend important people. Even Ben Franklin, one of the colonies' leading printers, published solidly conventional books. In fact, he printed books, one historian pointed out, "to make either money or friends, preferably both." Among Franklin's most popular titles were practical books such as his *Poor Richard's Almanack, Every Man His Own Doctor*, and the widely used schoolbook, *The New England Primer*. As with most other books printed in the colonies, these were not set in type until a certain number of people had already pledged to buy them. That, too, was a reason why most book printers took the safe route, avoiding offbeat ideas, unknown authors, and radical themes.

Letters were written on paper, folded, and sealed with a drop of hot wax. (Paper was too expensive to be wasted on envelopes.) Often the letters were written on one sheet, then turned upside down, and the writing continued between the lines, thus getting two pages of script onto a single sheet—however hard it might have been to read. Because there were no street numbers, the address might read something like this

---

*To: Miss Amanda Standish*
*Close to Long Wharf*
*On Thames Street*
*Newport, Rhode Island*

---

The writer of the letter would pay a fee to the person who agreed to deliver it. The letter might take a month or two to get to its destination, depending on the season (much longer in winter), the route, and the distance.

Although writing was not encouraged among slaves, many were taught (or laboriously taught themselves) how and wrote some memorable works. Chief

An early woodcut shows a post
rider announcing the arrival
of the mail and the news.

among these writers were two slaves from Boston. One,
Lucy Terry, is generally acknowledged as the first slave
poet. She began writing in 1746. The second was a
Boston house servant, Phyllis Wheatley, who published
a book of poems in 1773, when she was just twelve
years old.

In 1711 the English government set up a postal system for the colonies. It sputtered along until 1737 when Ben Franklin became one of two men appointed to run it. Franklin organized a group of men, called post riders, who carried the mail from one location to another. He also set fixed rates for postal deliveries. But in those days the cost of a letter was borne by the person who received it, not the one who wrote and mailed it!

Franklin also saw the establishment of a series of post roads that linked major cities and colonies together. (A highway that links Boston with New York even today is known as the Boston Post Road.) With that major improvement, the mails began to be delivered with some regularity.

Franklin also saw that the post riders carried newspapers as well as letters. This helped bring the colonies even closer together. For the first time, colonists in Rhode Island, for example, could learn what their counterparts in Maryland or Virginia or Pennsylvania were thinking by reading newspapers from those places.

# CHAPTER EIGHT

# Amusements

**I**n their amusements, as in most other aspects of their lives, colonial Americans made their own fun. That included adults as well as children, Native Americans as well as black slaves. And, despite the fact that everyone worked very hard simply to survive, people did find time to play games.

That was true of the fiercely religious Puritans of Massachusetts as well, although they did restrict some forms of entertainment. For example, they frowned on people putting on plays, dancing, sledding in the winter, and swimming in the summer.

Still, even the sternest Puritan leaders were not against people having *some* fun. They just didn't want people to make games and amusements too important a part of their lives. Or, as Cotton Mather, perhaps the strictest Puritan leader of all, put it, "Laudable recreations may be used now and then, but . . . let those recreations be used for sauce, not for meat."

Among Mather's "laudable recreations" were children's games, some of which are played even today with only minor changes from the way children in Massachusetts, Virginia, or Georgia played them hundreds of years ago. These included such games as tag, hide-and-seek (called "I Spy" in colonial times), and hop-scotch. Children then also played Blindman's Buff, sang to "Here We Go Round the Mulberry Bush" and "London Bridge Is Falling Down," and chanted counting-out rhymes.

In colonial times, Blindman's Buff was played this way. All the players stood in a circle around a room. One player was chosen to be "Buff." This player was blindfolded and led to the center of the room. A second player then began a conversation with Buff.

---

*How many horses has your father got?*
*Three [Buff answers]*
*What color are they?*
*Black, white, and gray [Buff says]*
*Turn about and turn about and catch whom you can*

---

Buff then spun around three times and tried to capture someone. When Buff did—and gave the name of the person caught—that player became Buff and the game continued.

Counting-out rhymes were used in another kind of children's game. In this one, all the players stood in a circle, hands outstretched. One player was chosen to be the "counter." That player walked around the circle chanting a counting-out rhyme, touching a hand with each word of the chant. The last player to be touched when the rhyme ended was declared out. The game went on until just one player remained.

Quite likely the best-known counting-out rhyme was this.

Colonial children at play

*Eeny, meeny, miney, moe,*
*Catch a tiger by the toe.*
*If he hollers let him go,*
*Eeny, meeny, miney, moe.*

Several other counting-out rhymes were used by colonial children in this game. These included

*Apples and oranges, two for a penny,*
*Takes a good scholar to count as many.*
*O-U-T, out goes she.*

and even nonsense rhymes like

*Ena, mena, mono, my,*
*Panalona, bona, stry,*
*Ee wee, fowl's neck*
*Hallibone, crackabone, ten and eleven,*
*O-U-T spells out, and out goes Y-O-U.*

Both boys and girls played these games, but, as in many other aspects of colonial life, boys had their games and sports, and girls had theirs. For example, there was "top-whipping," a favorite game of boys. A group of boys started their tops spinning at the same time. The boy whose top spun longest was declared the winner. Because the boys carved their own tops, it was a competition of whittling skills as well as top spinning.

Boys also played two different games of marbles. One of these was called "taw" after a line drawn in the dirt. Players shot a marble from behind the taw into a circle that held other marbles. The object was to knock the other marbles out of the circle. The second marble game involved digging a number of holes into the ground, then shooting a marble into each one.

Beyond these games, boys flew kites, climbed trees, and, in season, skated on ponds or went sledding or swimming, activities that were introduced into the colonies by Dutch settlers.

One visitor to Connecticut was so surprised at the number of young boys who took to sledding, he later wrote, "Every boy and youth in town from 8 to 18 had a little sledge, made with a rope, like a bridle, to the front by which it could be dragged after by one hand. . . . The driver would push off down the hill, as one would launch a boat, and then with the most astonishing velocity, precipitated by the weight of the owner, the little machine glided past and was at the lower end of the street in an instant."

While boys busied themselves with these and other

games, girls played mostly with dolls. These were usually carved from wood or were made from cornhusks or rags. One of the few outdoor sports colonial girls took part in was ice skating.

Another amusement colonial girls enjoyed was embroidering what are called "samplers." Samplers might include a border of the alphabet, some birds and flowers or trees, and a brief saying such as "In Adam's fall, We sinned all."

While considered an amusement, embroidering samplers could also become a time for teaching lessons. Depending on the whim of the teacher, a young girl might be required to rip out the thread one or more times until she got the stitches in the letter or design perfect, or at least up to her teacher's standards.

As children grew older, their games became more complicated. These included checkers, backgammon, dominoes, and cards, all played indoors.

Outside, besides the usual skating, sledding, and swimming, some forms of team sports (again, for boys) were gaining favor. These included cricket matches and games of rounders, an early form of today's baseball.

Without enough boys to make up teams for games like these, the boys might choose to play "One-oh-Cat," a very old game that traces its beginnings back to early England. In One-oh-Cat, a stake was driven into the ground until it stood about three feet high. Another stick, this one about a foot long, was placed atop the stake. A player would hit this second stick with an upward swing of a bat, sending the foot-long stick into

Colonial children knew a
number of indoor games,
including checkers.

the air. If the stick that was hit was caught in the air, the player who hit it was declared out. Otherwise, he ran to a base. If the stick was picked up and thrown, and hit the batter before he reached base, he was also out. If not, he stayed on base.

When the next batter hit the stick off the stake, the player on base would try to run back to the stake without being hit by the stick. If he made it, he got another turn at bat. If not, he changed positions with one of the players chasing the stick.

Some necessary kinds of work were turned into games and sport as well. These included hunting, fishing, and crabbing. Youngsters old enough to shoot (which meant all boys big enough to carry a musket) took part in shooting contests. They also fished for the largest cod or mackerel and tried to see who could trap the most crabs in a set amount of time.

Just as children and youngsters had their favorite amusements, so did adults. One of their favorite games was bowling. One bowling game involved rolling a small target ball on a lawn. Each player then rolled larger balls in turn. The object was to stop the larger ball as close to the target ball as possible.

A second kind of bowling was called nine pins. This game was introduced into the colonies by the Dutch. Nine wooden pins were set up in a pattern on a lawn. In turn, the players rolled balls to knock down the pins. The game became so popular that one colony, Connecticut, tried to ban it. The leaders of the colony believed people were gambling on the outcome.

The ban on ninepins did not stop the bowlers, however. They simply added a tenth pin, so it was no longer the game of nine pins! This game is still played in bowling alleys all across America today.

Quoits was another kind of game in which one object was tossed at a distant target. Quoits were metal rings tossed at an iron stake set in the ground. Points

Dances and dinner parties were
popular amusements, as shown in
this view of an elaborate 1700 ball.

were scored by ringing the stake or by being closest to
it. Quoits was popular with wealthy colonists. Those
who could not afford to buy a set of quoits used old
horseshoes instead. And it is horseshoes, not quoits,
which has come down to us today.

Some of the sports colonists took part in were quite

cruel. One of these was bull-baiting. Bull-baiting involved tying a bull to a stake and then teasing it unmercifully with hunting dogs. Another was cockfighting, quite popular in the southern colonies until it was outlawed. In this so-called sport, two specially trained roosters fought each other to the death.

As with games and sports for children and youngsters, adult women did not take part in any of these except for iceskating. Despite all the heavy work they did around the home all year round, women were considered too frail to participate!

As a result, women came into their own in home entertainment. The wealthier, upper-class women might organize a dance or an elaborate formal dinner for up to hundreds of guests. For the majority of women, however, home entertainment included such activities as playing musical instruments, dancing, and writing and acting in plays performed in their own homes. (Naturally, activities such as dancing and music and plays were frowned on in Puritan Massachusetts for many years. In fact, their effects are still felt to some degree in the so-called blue laws that forbid certain businesses from opening on Sundays and holidays.)

Nor did women lack opportunities to entertain in their homes. For one of the strong traits of colonial Americans, wealthy and poor alike, was their insistence on granting hospitality to strangers. Visitors from Europe often wrote about being greeted by Americans as if they were long-lost sons or daughters, something quite unusual in Europe. And with the presence of visitors, what better way to show off one's talents than by preparing a special meal, setting aside a room for the guests, and perhaps entertaining with a song or a play.

Native Americans enjoyed games and competitions of all kinds, especially gambling games involving rolling dice. They played these games for prizes such as blankets, furs, and tobacco pipes. Among their favorite sports was lacrosse (a popular sport in many high schools and colleges even today) and a game they called shinny, which was something similar to today's hockey. Whereas only men played lacrosse, women and children played games like double ball, hoops, and snow snakes.

In double ball, a curved stick was used to catch and throw a ball. Hoops involved tossing spears against

**Native Americans enjoyed footraces, canoe races, and other competitions.**

rolling hoops. Snow snakes, as the name suggests, was popular in the winter among Native Americans in the northern colonies. The "snake" was a stick, about five to nine feet long, the head of which was bent up and carved to look like a snake's head. Each snake was rubbed with a secret oil (known only to the owner of the snake), then flung down a track smoothed in the snow. The winning snake was the one that traveled the longest in the shortest amount of time.

Beyond games like these, Native Americans always liked to compete in footraces, hunting, fishing, and archery shooting.

The amusements of black slaves, especially those in the South, were not focused so much on sports, except perhaps for wrestling, hunting and fishing, and riding horses. They spent what free time they had telling stories, and occasionally dancing and playing any musical instruments they had. Like the white colonists, they also enjoyed barn raisings and corn huskings—events that ended with everyone participating in a food fest.

# Visiting Yesterday

Although it is enlightening to read about the way people lived in colonial times in America, it would be even more enjoyable to be able to experience close up what that kind of life was like. Fortunately, thanks to the efforts of government and individual people, we can do just that.

Every major city (and many small towns) in the thirteen original colonies has preserved examples of colonial life. These range in size from a section of a museum, to a single house or a municipal building, to neighborhoods and entire villages and towns. It is possible, for example, to wander through a settler's rude house, to gaze in wonder at the splendor of an early southern plantation house, to sit in a colonial schoolroom, or to walk the decks of a full-size replica of the *Mayflower*, the ship that brought the first Pilgrims to Plymouth, Massachusetts. Local historical societies in the cities and towns of the thirteen original colonies will point out places of special interest.

A painting from the Jamestown
foundation shows the flourishing
life of the colonial settlement.

Then there are cities and towns that are what might
be called "living museums." There you will find pockets
of colonial life tucked in among the hustle and bustle of
modern-day life. The Old Statehouse in Boston, for
example, or Charleston, South Carolina's Slave Market,

are two of hundreds of choices. In Newport, Rhode
Island, you can sit in a pew of a church where George
Washington once sat and listened to a sermon, or have
lunch at a table in a tavern more than a hundred years
*older* than the United States.

Finally, there are the grand historical sights, those
that show in great detail how life was lived before the
American Revolution. The best of these include Colo-

At Jamestown Festival Park, and at
other museum villages and restorations,
visitors can walk through the
streets of a colonial settlement.

nial Williamsburg, a painstakingly detailed museum of thirty-seven buildings. "Nowhere else in the world is it possible to go back so completely and authentically to another world as in Colonial Williamsburg," one visitor stated.

A second place of great interest in Williamsburg, Virginia, is the Jamestown Festival Park, which recreates the wattle and daub houses John Smith's adventurers built in 1608. Then there is Plimoth Plantation in Plymouth, Massachusetts, a faithful recreation of the original Pilgrim village. Here people dressed in the times go about life as if it were 1620.

Whether you visit Williamsburg or Philadelphia or a small town in the Carolinas, be sure to look up the historical sights, and then set aside some time to visit at least one or two. It will give you a new sense of appreciation for the people who risked so much to settle the colonies.

# Glossary

**apprenticeship** time during which a person learns a trade or art by working for a skilled person for little or no pay; apprenticeships were like trade or professional schools of today

**breechclout** loincloth worn by most Native American men made out of a piece of deer hide about one foot wide (metric) and several feet long; went between the legs and was tied around the waist with a leather thong; overlapping ends were usually decorated with beads or shells and hung down in front and back

**common room** another name for the kitchen in a seventeenth-century colonial home; the common room was dominated by a huge fireplace, often more than eight feet across the opening and five feet high

**cyphering** doing simple arithmetic problems such as adding, subtracting, multiplying, dividing

**doublet** close-fitting, waist-length jacket, usually of wool, worn by men; the sleeves of a doublet were often laced in rather than sewed, so they could be removed during warm weather

**dugout** crude shelter used by the first Dutch settlers in New Amsterdam; dugouts were large pits dug into the ground or into the side of a hill; the opening was covered with rough-cut wooden planks. Also: type of canoe used by Native Americans in the southern colonies; dugouts were fashioned from hollowed-out pine logs about twenty feet long and two to three feet wide

**hardtack** hard, dry biscuit made with flour and water, which served as bread on sailing ships

**homespun clothing** clothing made at home, especially clothing of linen or wool, which was spun into yarn and thread and woven into cloth on a small hand loom

**hominy** kernels of dried hulled corn, cooked as a cereal or as a dish to accompany meat

**hornbook** page with the alphabet and the Lord's Prayer, covered with a thin sheet of transparent horn and fastened to a wooden frame shaped like a paddle; hornbooks were used in teaching reading to children

**johnnycake** fried bread made from cornmeal and milk, sometimes with molasses and salt as well; often called "journey cake" because travelers would pack a few to eat on a trip

**lean-to** simple, three-sided shelter, usually made of tree limbs and woven grass, built against a tree or a post; the fourth side was left open to the weather

**longhouse** a long communal dwelling, especially of the Iroquois Indians

**post-rider** mail carrier who rode a horse along a mail route called a post road; riders delivered all mail to inns along the post road; people who expected letters went to the inn to pick them up; they also paid the postage, not the person who sent the letter

**saltbox** type of house two or two-and-a-half stories in front with a long roof that sloped down nearly to the ground in the back; so called because its shape was similar to the boxes salt was stored in

**samp** porridge, or thick soup, made from coarse cornmeal boiled alone with milk or cooked with beans or peas and salt pork

**sampler** piece of cloth decorated with ornamental stitches showing alphabet, birds, or flowers, to show needlework skills; embroidering samplers was an important part of every girl's education

**shallop** small, light, open boat propelled by a sail or oars, or both

**stocks** device for punishment made of heavy timbers with holes to lock in ankles and, sometimes, wrists; stocks were similar to a **pillory**, another device for punishment; the pillory had a wooden frame with holes for the neck and hands; people confined to a pillory stood, while those in stocks sat

**voider** woven basket into which everything used in eating a meal, including cloth napkins, was put, to be taken away and washed before the next meal

**wattle and daub** building material consisting of tree branches and sticks woven together (the wattle) and plastered with mud (the daub); used in enclosing the walls in early homes

**wigwam** temporary one-room hut made of dome-shaped framework of branches covered with tree bark, woven mats, or animal skins; wigwams were the principal homes of the Algonquian Indian nation and were copied by many early European settlers

# Bibliography

---
**BOOKS**

Alderman, Clifford Lindsey. *The Story of the Thirteen Colonies*. New York: Random House, 1966.

Andrews, Charles M. *Colonial Folkways*. New Haven: Yale University Press, 1919, 1946, 1975.

Bailey, Carolyn Sherwin. *Children of the Handcrafts*. New York: Viking, 1935.

Baldwin, Gordon C. *How Indians Really Lived*. New York: G. P. Putnam's, 1967.

Barck & Lefler. *Colonial America*. New York: Macmillan, 1968.

Bjorkland, Karnal. *Indians of Northwestern America*. New York: Dodd, Mead, 1909.

Boorstin, Daniel J. *Americans: The Colonial Experience*. New York: Random House, 1958.

Booth, Sally Smith. *Seeds of Anger: Revolts in America 1607–1771*. New York: Hastings House, 1977.

Bridenbaugh, Carl. *The Colonial Craftsman.* Chicago: University of Chicago Press, 1950.

Brown, Richard D. *Massachusetts: A History.* New York: W. W. Norton, 1978.

Burke, Helen Newbury. *Foods From the Founding Fathers.* Norris, Tennessee Exposition Press, 1978.

Carson, Jane. *Colonial Virginians at Play.* Colonial Williamsburg Foundation, 1989.

Coleman, R. V. *The First Frontier.* New York: Scribner's, 1948.

Divine, Breen & Frederickson. *America Past and Present.* Glenview, Illinois: Scott, Foresman, 1984.

Earle, Alice Morse. *Customs and Fashions in Old New England.* New York: Scribner's, 1893.

————. *Home Life in Colonial Days.* New York: Macmillan, 1902.

Escher, Jr., Franklin. *A Brief History of the United States.* New York: New American Library, 1954, 1962.

Fisher, Leonard Everett. *The Schoolmaster.* New York: Franklin Watts, 1967.

Fisher, Margaret, et al. *Colonial America.* Baltimore: The Fideler Co., 1974.

Fradin, Dennis. *The Thirteen Colonies.* Chicago: Childrens Press, 1988.

Glubok, Shirley, ed. *Home and Child Life in Colonial Days.* New York: Macmillan, 1969.

Goodwin, Maud Wilder. *Dutch and English on the Hudson.* New Haven: Yale University Press, 1919.

Greene, Lorenzo Johnston. *The Negro in Colonial New England.* New York: Columbia University Press, 1968.

Grunfeld, Frederic V., ed. *Games of the World.* New York: Holt, 1975.

Hawke, David Freeman. *Everyday Life in Early America.* New York: Harper & Row, 1988.

Keller, Allan. *Colonial America: A Compact History.* Wheeling, Illinois: Hawthorne Books, 1971.

Loeper, John J. *Going to School in 1776*. New York: Atheneum, 1973.

Madison, Arnold. *How the Colonists Lived*. New York: David McKay, 1981.

McGovern, Anne. *. . . If You Lived in Colonial Times*. New York: Four Winds Press, 1964.

Miers, Earl Schenck. *A Blazing Star*. Chicago: Rand McNally, 1970.

Morrisgost, Ira. *Our American Colonists*. Philadelphia: Davis, 1942.

Morison, Samuel Eliot. *The Story of the Old Colony of New Plymouth*. New York: Knopf, 1956.

Peck, Ira B. *A Genealogical History of the Descendants of Joseph Peck*. Alfred Mudge & Sons, 1868.

Phipps, Frances. *Colonial Kitchens: Their Furnishings and Their Gardens*. Wheeling, Illinois: Hawthorne, 1972.

Starke, Marion L. *Land Where Our Fathers Died*. New York: Doubleday, 1962.

Tannahill, Renny. *Food in History*. New York: Stein & Day, 1973.

Tunis, Edwin. *Colonial Craftsmen*. Winter Park, Florida: World Publishing, 1965.

_____. *Shaw's Fortune*. Winter Park, Florida: World Publishing, 1966.

_____. *Colonial Living*. Winter Park, Florida: World Publishing, 1957.

Vaughn, Alden T., ed. *America Before the Revolution*. Englewood Cliffs, New Jersey: Prentice-Hall, 1967.

Wertenbaker, Thomas J. *The Age of Colonial Culture*. New York: New York University Press, 1949.

Wilson, George F. *Saints and Strangers*. Reynal & Hitchcock, 1945.

Wright, Louis B. *History of the Thirteen Colonies*. New York: American Heritage Publishing, 1967.

Ziner, Feeny. *The Pilgrims and Plymouth Colony*. New York: American Heritage Publishing, 1966.

## PERIODICALS

Bulger, Margery. "Ali Ali in Free . . ." *Early American Life* (August 1975).

Hooker, Margaret Huntington. "Early American Cookery." American Review, 1981.

Hume, Ivor Noel. "First Look at a Lost Virginia Settlement." *National Geographic* (June 1975).

Miller, Margo. "The Way We Were at Home: 1750–1870." *The Boston Globe*, 16 November 1990.

## ALSO

Various unpublished papers, journals, diaries, etc., in the archives of the Redwood Library, Newport, Rhode Island; the Rhode Island Historical Society, Providence, Rhode Island; the Newport Preservation Society, Newport, Rhode Island; and the University of Virginia, Charlottesville, Virginia.

# Index

# About the Author

John F. Warner is a writer of children's books, who also develops educational materials. He lives in Newport, Rhode Island.